Remember Him

D1483932

Remember Him

J. W. Alexander

THE BANNER OF TRUTH TRUST

THE BANNER OF TRUTH TRUST
3 Murrayfield Road, Edinburgh EH12 6EL, UK
P O Box 621, Carlisle, Pennsylvania 17013, USA

*

© The Banner of Truth Trust 2000

First published in 1854 by
Anson D. F. Randolph & Co., New York

First Banner of Truth Edition 2000

ISBN 0 85151 790 0

*

Typeset in 11/13 pt OldStyle 7 at
The Banner of Truth Trust, Edinburgh
Printed in Great Britain by
The Bath Press

Contents

Contents

Preface

This little book is not a treatise on the Lord's Supper and it is not intended to rival or supersede larger works on that subject. It has its origin in a desire to provide young communicants with fuller advice than can, in ordinary cases, be given orally to individuals by their pastor and its latter part is related to the beginnings of a Christian walk. Small and plain though this work is, it may also be useful to Christians of some standing in the Church, especially those who have been without careful instruction.

The writer has employed a mode of direct address which may seem discourteous and unfeeling. However, he has adopted it deliberately because it produces three important qualities in a collection of writings, namely, clarity, brevity, and pointedness. The passages of Scripture which are cited have been selected with some care. The reader will gain by looking them up, and even by committing them to memory.

He humbly dedicates this effort to God, with the earnest prayer that it may be made a blessing to all who read it.

J. W. ALEXANDER

1. *The Aim of this Book*

You have now taken the first solemn step which is to separate you from the world. You have vowed to follow Christ and to be numbered among his people. In these circumstances and if you have rightly been affected by him, you are conscious of a tender fear of doing wrong and an earnest desire to be instructed. The following paragraphs have been written to provide you with some clear directions about what is involved in professing Christ and what are its consequent obligations.

2. *The Lord's Supper*

The duty of confessing Christ before men rests on every one who hears the Gospel. It is spoken of in Scripture in immediate connection with saving faith. 'If thou shalt confess with thy mouth the Lord Jesus, and shalt believe in thine heart that God hath raised him from the dead, thou shalt be saved' (*Rom.* 10:9). In the same way, the duty of commemorating the death of Christ at his table is binding on all who have come to know his gracious work. While impenitence and unbelief disqualify people from a proper observance of the Supper, they provide no excuse for its neglect because to have no faith and love to express, is a sin in itself.

3. *The Nature of the Sacrament*

The Lord's Supper was instituted by our blessed
Saviour, on the night before he was betrayed; and you
will do well to read with care the record of its institution
in Matthew 26:17–35; Mark 14:12–26; Luke 22:7–39 and
1 Corinthians 11:23–34. It is a sacrament, that is, a holy
ordinance which signifies, seals, and exhibits the benefits
of Christ's mediation to those who are within the
covenant of grace. It has an outward sign and it signifies
a spiritual grace. The outward sign is bread and wine,
given and received, according to Christ's appointment.
The inward grace is the communication, by the Holy
Spirit and according to his sovereign pleasure, of such
faith, comfort, and spiritual nourishment as are in keeping with the reception of Christ, slain for our sins. This
visible action of the Supper shows forth his death, and
believers engage in it, as obeying his dying injunction,
'This do in remembrance of me' (*Luke* 22:19).

4. *The Doctrine of the Sacrament*

The Sacrament of the Lord's Supper exhibits, in plain
action, a great doctrine, which is also conveyed in words.
Unless you understand this, you must fail to derive
spiritual nourishment by feeding on the Lord's body and
blood. This doctrine is the Atonement. It should be

graven on the tablets of the mind and heart. Ponder deeply , therefore, the following truths: When the fulness of time had come, the eternal Son of God, co-equal with the Father, took upon himself our human nature, with all its infirmities, yet without sin. The Word was made flesh, and the two natures were inseparably joined together in one Person, who is Christ the Mediator. The Lord Jesus was made under the law, perfectly fulfilled it, obeying its precept and exhausting its penalty. In his humiliation he suffered most grievous anguish of soul and most painful agonies of body; he was crucified, he died, and was laid in the tomb. By his perfect sacrifice of himself, he fully satisfied Divine justice, and purchased reconciliation and eternal glory for all those whom the Father had given to him. The entire benefits of this redemption are offered to you in the Gospel, and more summarily and vividly in this sacrament, and your title to them becomes sure when you believe on the Lord Jesus Christ.

5. *Benefits to be Expected*

You are therefore called to this memorial by love to Christ, and a consequent desire to obey his affecting command. If you find grace to partake in a right spirit, you will derive special benefits. You will, in the exercise of faith upon the Redeemer here strikingly represented, feed upon his body and blood, not in any physical sense, but as receiving and applying to yourself Christ crucified and all the benefits of his death. This sacrament thus becomes one of the means of salvation, not from any power in itself, but by the operation of the Holy Spirit and the blessing of Christ. The approach to his table which you are contemplating is, then, one of the most solemn acts of your life, and is not to be attempted without much reflection, inquiry, and prayer.

6. Admission to Full Communion

As the Lord's Supper represents the great object of saving faith, it is impossible for one who has no faith to partake of it in a proper or acceptable manner. This is a matter for your own inquiry. Christ's ministers and other church-officers cannot read the heart. They must be governed by evidences taken from your words and conduct. They may approve your knowledge and life and your inward experience, but they cannot pronounce you to be regenerate; and do not do so by admitting you to sealing ordinances. Their warrant for so admitting you is not the certainty of your conversion, which they cannot know, but only the credibility of your profession of faith in Christ, which they must judge from your words and actions. You should therefore be solemnly warned against the disastrous error of taking your admission to the communion as a part of the evidence that you are really a child of God. That evidence is to be derived from a careful comparison of your heart and life with the marks of grace laid down in the Scriptures.

7. *Improper Motives*

If you believe that this sacrament is saving in itself; if you expect benefit from mere outward participation in it; if you seek to declare yourself better than others; if you desire to gain a reputation for goodness among men; or if you use it as a means of furthering any worldly purpose, you are drawing near to this sacrament on false grounds.

8. *Why Should I Partake?*

You should ask yourself why you propose to come to the Lord's Table. If rightly disposed, your answer must be something like this to be sufficient: Because I believe in the Lord Jesus, because I love him, and because I wish to remember him as my dying Redeemer: not because I am good, but in the deep persuasion that I am a sinner. As a sinner, relying on his righteousness, receiving his promise, and hoping for his Spirit, I desire to sit at the foot of his cross. As ignorant and wavering, I crave new faith, in this holy ordinance. As his child and servant, I long to come out from the world, and make the most public avowal of my attachment and subjection to him. And as a Christian, I would hasten to own my fellowship and unity with that body, of which this bread and wine are the communion.

9. Causes of Fear

An extraordinary dread of approaching the Lord's Table exists in many minds. This is partly caused by a misunderstanding of certain words of the Apostle Paul, and it must be removed by considering their true meaning. The expressions are found in his account of the institution. 'Wherefore, whosoever shall eat this bread and drink this cup of the Lord unworthily, shall be guilty of the body and blood of the Lord . . . For he that eateth and drinketh unworthily, eateth and drinketh damnation [the word means *judgement*] to himself, not discerning the Lord's body' (*1 Cor.* 11:27,29).

It is so important to determine who are those declared to be guilty and under judgment. For this purpose we must examine the history and context of the passage. Paul was writing to the Corinthians. They had fallen into such gross abuses of the Lord's Supper as annulled its real character (*1 Cor.* 11:20). They turned it into a common banquet, where each ate his own food and drank to excess. It was this which was eating and drinking 'unworthily' and which brought on them guilt and condemnation. But these censures do not apply to fearful souls, in our day, who come reverently to the ordinance, even if it they should come without having prepared themselves fully.

10. Warning

At the same time, we should not draw near without a holy awe because there are abuses and profanations of this sacrament which fall short of the riotous enormities of Corinth. God's displeasure falls on him who rushes to this table, ignorant of its true intent and of the way of salvation; unprepared and careless, without solemnity and a desire to have right views of it; hard, impenitent, and indulging himself in known sin.

11. May Doubting Souls Come?

The profession which you make here is of faith in Christ and not of assurance of hope. That distinction is important. If, therefore, you feel your sins and long to be delivered from them; if you attempt and pray to be enabled to come in faith; if you cast yourself on the righteousness of Christ, you need not dread the judgements threatened in Scripture. Hence it would be wrong to defer your profession of faith until you receive the grace of assurance. This is well and soundly expressed by the Westminster Assembly of Divines: 'One who doubteth of his being in Christ, or of his due preparation to the sacrament of the Lord's supper, may have true interest in Christ, though he be not yet assured thereof; and in God's account hath it, if he be duly affected with the apprehension of the want of it, and unfeignedly desires to be found in Christ, and to depart from iniquity: in which case (because promises are made, and this sacrament is appointed, for the relief even of weak and doubting Christians) he is to bewail his unbelief, and labour to have his doubts resolved; and, so doing, he may and ought to come to the Lord's Supper, that he may be further strengthened' (*Larger Catechism,* Answer to Question 172).

12. Insufficient Reasons for Delay

Even among those who cherish a persuasion that they are born of God, there are some who debar themselves from coming to the table. They plead that it is possible to live as a Christian without making a public declaration of it; that they are not yet acknowledged by the world as reformed persons; that cases of apostasy are numerous; that they fear lest they should dishonour their profession, or that they wish to subject themselves to a long course of trial. In many cases, these reasons are prompted by a secret unwillingness to take up the cross. When the love of Christ is in the heart, it ought to be made public by an open confession. In the early Church there was no such thing as owning Christ and yet living separately from his people. There is danger in postponing this public act on superficial grounds, and some have been known to linger like this all their days. If there is sin in hasty profession, there is also sin in neglecting the dying command of Jesus; and if fear of the world's opinion be the motive, his threatening should be well considered: 'For whosoever shall be ashamed of me and of my words, of him shall the Son of Man be ashamed when he shall come in his own glory, and in his Father's, and of the holy angels' (*Luke* 9:26).

13. Imperfect Views of the Ordinance

Some persons seem to never acquire a distinct notion of the Lord's Supper in its essential nature. There are certain things implied in it, and flowing from it, which nevertheless are not its grand peculiarity and character- istic. These confused ideas are encouraged by some of our familiar phrases. For example, few expressions are more common in reference to the communion, than that of 'joining the Church' but this is only incidental to it. Indeed, it is baptism that is the rite of initiation and not the eucharist. We do, in fact, join ourselves to the Lord's people: but this is not the primary idea. Similarly, a 'profession of religion' is spoken of, and so the resolve to lead a holy life; but this also is secondary, and not included in the rite as such. Again, though it seals to believers the benefits of the Covenant of Grace, the Lord's Supper is not itself a covenant. The notion of vow or compact does not enter into the original idea. Great evils will be avoided, if you fix your thoughts first on that view which is first in the institution itself. It is a remem- bering of Christ – a showing forth of the Lord's death – a feeding on his body and blood - and a communion with his people. These should be the precise object of our contemplations while the other aspects, properly guarded, are not to be rejected.

14. Encouragements

Great blessings are derived from being a conscientious communicant. As has already been said, you will find confirmation of faith and all graces at this sacrament. You will be honoured and comforted by the fellowship of Christ's people; you will be enclosed, and protected, and watched over, in the fold; you will in a higher degree enjoy the acquaintance, sympathy, converse, and prayers of true Christians; you will have facility, stimulus, aid, and example in holy living; and you will hold forth the word of life to the unconverted world, in a manner which would not otherwise be possible. To all which may be added, the indescribable comfort of a consciousness that you are obeying him who died for you.

15. Need of Self-Knowledge

Overseers in the church, as has been said, can only judge whether your profession of faith should be believed. But there is a secret matter between God and your own soul, which must now engage your most careful attention. Everything in this ordinance implies the presence of a new heart. Even if you should escape the greater condemnation of the sacrilegious, you cannot partake of spiritual food, in an unregenerate state. Hence the manifest importance of an immediate and thorough inquiry into your condition, as a condemned or a justified soul. 'Let a man examine himself, and so let him eat of this bread and drink of this cup' (*1 Cor.* 11:28).

16. Self-Examination

Though it is assumed that you have already tested yourself, you should scrutinise your experience even more deeply before going to the table of our Lord. And how greatly do you need the aid of the Holy Spirit to do this! It should be your maxim, that no marks of evidence are of the slightest value which are not clearly laid down in the Word of God. Many such tests have been invented. You should next be aware that the great difficulty is not in laying down marks, but in identifying them in yourself. Volumes have been written on this single subject. One undoubted fruit of the Spirit, in the heart, standing out bright and undeniable is suffcent ground for belief that the soul is regenerate. But we are prone to mistake, sometimes in our own favour and sometimes against our hopes. Observe carefully, therefore, that in the helps about to be given, it is not thought that the topic is exhausted. What follows is rather an example of the way in which this inquiry may be conducted.

17. Questions Before the Communion[1]

Have I seen myself to be, by nature and by practice, a lost and helpless sinner? Have I seen not only the sinfulness of particular acts and omissions, but that my heart is a seat and fountain of sin, and that in me, as unrenewed, there is no good thing? Has a view of this led me to despair of help from myself, and to see that I must be altogether indebted to Christ for salvation, and to the gracious aid of the Holy Spirit for strength and ability to perform my duty?

On what is my hope of acceptance with God founded? On my reformation? on my sorrow for sin? on my prayers? on my tears? on my good works and religious

[1]These questions are partly based on a series drawn up by Dr William Henry Green of Princeton.

observances? or on Christ alone, as my all in all? Has Christ ever appeared very precious to me? Have I ever felt great freedom in committing my soul to him? If I have done this, has it been not only to be delivered from the punishment due to sin, but also from the power, pollution, dominion, and very existence of sin within me?

Do I hate all sin, and desire to be delivered from it, without any exception of a favourite lust? Do I pray much to be delivered from sin? Do I strive against it? Do I avoid temptation? Do I, in any measure, obtain the victory over sin? Have I so repented of it, that my soul is really set against it?

Have I counted the cost of following Christ, or of being truly religious? Am I ready to be detached from empty pleasures, from the indulgence of my lusts, and from a sinful conformity to the world? Can I face ridicule, contempt, and serious opposition? In the view of these things, am I willing to take up the cross, and to follow Christ wherever he shall lead me? Is it my solemn purpose, in reliance on his gracious aid, to cleave to him and to his cause and people, to the end of life?

Do I love holiness? Do I earnestly desire to be more and more conformed to God and to his holy law, to bear more and more the likeness of my Redeemer? Am I resolved, in God's strength, to endeavour conscientiously to perform my whole duty, to God, to my neighbour, and to myself?

Do I conscientiously offer secret prayer daily? Do I ever experience delight in it? Have I a set time, and place, and order of exercises for performing this duty? Is it my purpose, as the head of a household, to maintain the worship of God in my family? Do I read a portion of the Holy Scriptures every day, and in a devout manner? Do I love the Bible? Do I ever perceive a sweetness in its truths? Do I find them suited to my necessities, and do I at times see a wonderful beauty, excellence, and glory in God's Word? Do I take it as the 'man of my counsel' [*Psa.* 119:24, margin], and endeavour to have both heart and life conformed to its demands?

Have I given myself away to God, solemnly and irrevocably, hoping for acceptance through Christ alone, and taking God in Christ, as the covenant God and satisfying portion of my soul? Does the glory of God appear to me the first, greatest, and best of all objects?

Have I such a love to mankind as was unknown to me before? Have I a great desire that the souls of men should be saved, by being brought to the Redeemer? Do I feel a peculiar love to God's people, because they bear their Saviour's image? Am I at peace with every fellow Christian? If not, have I made endeavours to be reconciled? Do I, from the heart forgive all who have wronged me? Do I desire and endeavour to grow in grace and in the knowledge of Christ my Saviour, more and more? Am I willing to sit at his feet as a little child, and to submit my understanding implicitly to his teaching, imploring his Spirit to guide me into all necessary truth, to save me from all fatal errors, to enable me to receive the truth in the love of it, and to transform me more and more into a likeness of himself?

Do I love the Lord Jesus Christ? Do I especially love him as dying for my sins? Do I desire to remember him, in this his dying love, at his table? Am I sufficiently acquainted with the nature and design of this sacrament? Have I carefully considered the history of our Lord's sufferings, in the four Gospels? Have I diligently read the accounts of this institution, in the New Testament? Am I ready, as a sinner redeemed by this blood, to go to this ordinance? Am I desirous of communion in it with Christ's people? Am I willing to submit myself to the government and discipline of the Church? Do I feel it to be important to adorn Christian profession by a holy, exemplary, amiable, and blameless walk? Do I fear to bring a reproach on the cause of Christ? Am I afraid of backsliding, and of being left to return to a state of carelessness and indifference in religion? Have I any sufficient reason for withholding the profession of my faith? And what is my duty, in consideration of the possibility that I may be summoned into eternity before another communion service?

18. Difficulty of the Work

The greatest care is necessary in an affair so important as the examination of your state before God. You will naturally be reluctant to come to an unfavourable conclusion about this and so self-love combined with self-ignorance will expose you to the danger of self-deception. Earnestly endeavour to exercise a holy candour. Be thorough and, for this purpose, do not be hasty in your search but use frequent repetition. Insert the probe fully, even though it reach the quick. Mingle prayer to God with your self-examination, and this for two reasons; first, because in acts of devotion, both sins and graces are most likely to come to light, and secondly, because God only can reveal you to yourself. Let your cry be 'Search me, O God, and know my heart; try me, and know my thoughts; and see if there be any wicked way in me; and lead me in the way everlasting' (*Psa.* 139:23–24).

But special counsel is necessary for those who tend to form adverse judgements of their own state. Realise that you are looking for the reality and not the perfection, or even eminence of piety. Life exists in the infant as well as the robust man. Remember that all graces are not always developed in the same degree. Do not be misled by the experience of others. There is infinite diversity in the operations of the Spirit. Do not yield to alarm because you do not have the feelings which others have, or any certain order of exercises; but let the sure Word of God alone be your scales, standard, and touchstone.

19. Undue Fears

There is a godly fear which befits approach to this sacrament but there is no benefit from a legal and slavish dread, which is often made up of self-righteousness and superstition. The best cure for this is to have the heart sprinkled from an evil conscience by the blood of Christ (*Heb.* 10:22). Terror does not belong to the Lord's Supper, which you should consider as a feast of love. The Lord Jesus himself invites you, where he has promised to be present (*Matt.* 18:20). Deliberately consider with what feelings you would enter a room, if you knew that the blessed Saviour in his visible humanity was waiting to receive you. He was often thus approached. Did he reject, or frown on the Syrophoenician woman, or the sinful woman at Simon's house, or the woman taken in adultery? (*Mark* 7:24–30; *Luke* 8:36-50; *John* 8:1–11) 'This man', it was said, 'receiveth sinners'. And he is 'Jesus Christ, the same yesterday, today and for ever' (*Heb* .13:8).

20. *Preparation*

The whole period between conversion and communion may be regarded as preparation. So solemn a matter as coming to the Lord's table may well demand special engagement of the thoughts, and, where the work of grace has been deep, it is the one great subject which has reigned over the mind during these weeks or months. From the moment when you determined to profess your faith until the moment when this purpose is carried out , it is difficult to conceive how this one topic can ever be absent from your reflections for many minutes at once. Take all the time which is at your disposal for devotional exercises connected with the coming ordinance. If your feelings express themselves in frequent and almost constant prayer, it will be well. Self-examination must not exclude more fruitful exercises. The sacrament exhibits sublime facts, doctrines, and blessings: let these engage your meditations. Bring fully before your mind the scene of our Lord's betrayal, agony, and death; for it is this which you are to remember. Instead of human descriptions, read and ponder the simple narratives of the Scriptures. (*Matt.* 26:36–75; 27:1–66; *Mark* 14:26–72; 15:1–47; *Luke* 22:47–71; 23:1–56 and *John* 18:19) Think upon these, until the heart is melted. Be not content with the stirring of natural feelings but yield to sorrow for your sins, which were thus expiated. Express yourself in acts of faith to the Lord Jesus Christ personally, as dying on the cross for you. And let love embrace and enjoy him, gratitude praise him, and the spirit of self-oblation carry you out of yourself, in unconditional surrender. Thus feeling, you will be prepared for the holy table.

21. Congregational Preparation

Customs vary in different congregations, but it is generally the case that some public services are held during the week preceding the Lord's Supper. These are great aids to private piety and to the culture of brotherly affection. Forsake them not, 'as the manner of some is' (*Heb.* 10:25). In your attendance upon them, seek to derive the blessings promised to the faithful use of ordinances.

22. First Communion

Although the first occasion of drawing near to the Lord's Table is likely to be ever remembered, it is not always marked with eminent spiritual peace or joyfulness. Indeed it is common to hear sad lamentations, and sometimes expressions bordering on utter despondency after the solemn rite is over. This result is caused partly by incorrect or exaggerated expectations of immediate comfort, and partly by the very trepidation of the mind when placed in novel and trying circumstances. It is useful therefore to be taught that acceptable participation in this sacrament is not always evidenced by high or rapturous emotions. But to avoid the opposite evil, you should seek for calmness of mind, as a most important condition of benefit. If self-examination has been faithful, you may freely give yourself up, on the morning of the Lord's day, to serene and tranquil waiting. In plain terms, do not try to think of too many things. Realise that you are not to give, but to receive. Place your soul in an expectant posture. It is impossible to wait for influences of the Holy Spirit without a certain degree of composure, self-possession, and holy stillness. Seat yourself, so to speak, at the foot of the cross.

23. Simple Views

The Lord's Supper has sometimes been called an 'epitome of the gospel'. This is because, in a certain sense, the doctrine which it presents is the central truth of that gracious system in which all truths harmonise and toward which all lines converge. But this expression may mislead and embarrass the inexperienced soul by causing it to attempt a comprehensive view of all the various truths which are in any way involved in this ordinance. Now it is a law of the human mind that it cannot be fully occupied with more than one object at the same time and it is equally true, that this object, in order to affect the feelings, must be held for some time before the thoughts. Hence the wisdom of concentrating your contemplations, as much as possible, upon the grand peculiar truth held forth in the sacrament; and on that principal duty to which you are called, namely, the remembrance of Christ, and the showing forth his death. Other subordinate truths will best range themselves under this.

24. Preliminary Services

The Lord's Supper is commonly preceded by the usual worship and instructions of the Lord's Day, modified by reference to the approaching ordinance. It is to be hoped that the day will never come when it shall be allowed in our assemblies, as in some others, for this sacrament to be treated as a mere appendage and for there to be no special allusion in the preceding sermon and devotions to the atoning work of Christ. It is natural, and it is usual, for all the public services of the day to have a marked reference to expiation and dying love. To these services, you will be disposed to give your reverent attention. But here experience shows that you need a warning. Perhaps the train of thought presented in the ministry, and the emotions aroused, differ from those which you looked for, and which you have been trying to entertain. If so, make no effort to resist this new leaning of soul. It may be the very answer to your prayers, and the very state of mind which you most need. For the minister of the sanctuary is under a providential and gracious guidance, with respect to God's people.

25. Feelings Suited
to the Ordinance

The operations of the mind are rapid; many thoughts and feelings may be compressed into a single instant. During the most interesting service therefore, there will be many ideas in addition to those suggested by the minister. There is therefore a discretion to be observed, in cherishing, suppressing, or directing such thoughts; for upon these will depend the temper of the soul. By a due exercise of the faculty of attention, we may hold certain objects before the mind, and thus indirectly promote certain feelings. The emotions which are proper during a sacramental service are such as these: Lowliness in the presence of the God of infinite majesty, whom you have offended, and who yet invites you to his table. Sorrow for sin, and sympathetic tenderness, in consideration of the sufferings of Jesus in your stead. Faith in Christ, as the Lamb of God, once laid upon the altar, and now significantly offered to you in the sacrament. Filial confidence in him, as freely pardoning all your sins. Melting love to the Redeemer, as the chiefest among ten thousand and altogether lovely. Absolute dedication to him, in thankful offering of yourself, to be his for evermore. Sincere affection to God's people, who now surround you in fellowship. Any one of these feelings is right, and not to be driven away or repressed. And if during the solemnity you find your thoughts and feelings borne away into new avenues, altogether different from anything which you had been prescribing to yourself, yet in general agreement with the intent of the ordinance; be not afraid to yield to such suggestions, which may proceed from the Spirit of all good.

26. Christ Present

There is perhaps no one thought more suited to prepare and compose the mind, than this, that the Lord Jesus is present at his own table. Make the endeavour to grasp this as a reality. Look towards him as the one object; with the assurance that he is just as tender, compassionate, and forgiving, as when he was on earth; and that he is the most accessible being in the universe. Rejoice that he knows all things, and looks to the very bottom of your heart. Confide to him your deepest sense of unworthiness, and of your unfitness for this privilege; and flee to his righteousness in this solemn moment, as fully covering all your sins. Guard against the supposition, that your acceptance is dependent on feelings of joy or even comfort, at his table. Go out of yourself, and place your whole heart in his hands. If your thoughts wander or become confused, if you find yourself suddenly cold and hard or even bereft of all right feelings, avoid struggles of mind to repair the evil; but gently bring back your thoughts to the all-gracious and present Jesus, who sees and pities your infirmities.

27. *The Administration*

Although we reject the belief in any consecration as changes the nature of the elements, we hold the moment of administering the rite to be very solemn. The sacramental actions are divinely appointed; they are significant; and they are addressed to the senses. They should therefore be attentively and reverently observed. Look at the bread broken, and the wine poured out; for herein are emblematically shown the breaking of that sacred body, and the shedding of that precious blood. Look through them to the dying and atoning Saviour; this is 'discerning the Lord's body' (*1 Cor.* 11:29). Open your ears and heart to the truth which may be uttered from the word of God. Thus shall you be in readiness for the actual participation. The entire series of actions, during which the bread and wine are given and received, with suitable words, is to be considered as sacramental; but the most solemn moment is that in which you individually receive the elements.

28. *The Act of Partaking*

The act of partaking is passing and brief. The thoughts of those few instants must of course be short. It is plain therefore that your views at thus juncture must be extremely simple. You will not greatly err, if you fix your regards on 'Jesus Christ, and him crucified' (*1 Cor.* 2:2). Such childlike thoughts as these will properly arise:

'Lord Jesus, I remember thee!'

'Jesus, Saviour, I here remember thy body broken for my sins.'

'Lamb of God, who takest away the sin of the world, have mercy upon me!'

'Lord, I show forth thy death till thou come!'

'O Lord Jesus Christ, I take this up in memory of thee, as the new covenant in thy blood!'

'I, a wretched sinner, confide in thy blood, shed for many for the remission of sins.' 'Lord, I believe, help thou mine unbelief!'

'Blessed Jesus, who hast died for me, I here give myself away to thee!'

'God be merciful to me a sinner!'

'Let this cup of blessing be blessed unto me, for the sake of my dying Lord, whom I thus remember!'

Any one of these short prayers would be appropriate and edifying; and the sacred calm of the soul should not be interrupted by ingenious attempts to vary or multiply the thoughts. Indeed the soul that silently waits on God, must leave a portion of its activity, at such a time, to the suggestions of the Holy Spirit.

29. *Thoughts of Self and Sin*

During the progress of the ordinance, the mind will necessarily turn inward. Be not discouraged if all there seems dark and repulsive. It is as a guilty helpless creature that you have come to this table. You may justly cry, 'Unclean, unclean!' (*Lev.* 13:45). The sins which crucified him whom your soul loves may well seem bitter and horrible, as you gaze on the cross. The most profound humiliation is compatible with faith and love. Should you vow an everlasting separation from your sins, it will be with good reason. Indeed the moment is most favourable for inflicting deadly wounds on the body of sin.

30. *Thoughts of Christ*

The great object of your thoughts is however, the Master of the feast, the Lord Jesus, here 'evidently set forth crucified' (*Gal.* 3:1). When he is vividly before your mind, in his agonies and death, believe on him, rest in him, cleave to him. By faith feed on him, as 'the Bread of life' (*John* 6:48, 51, 53, 56). Do not hesitate to let the full tide of your affections flow out to him. Love him, as infinitely holy and gracious. 'Set to your seal that God is true' (*John.*3:33) and appropriate him as yours; saying, 'My Lord, and my God!' (*John* 20:28). Adore the ineffable glory of God as it shines in the fact of Jesus Christ. And renew your covenant, by yielding yourself irrevocably to him, as your Lord and King. These are but examples of the acts of a happy soul in communion with Christ at his Table.

31. *Thoughts of Brethren*

As your eye wanders towards the brethren, who, side by side with you, sit at the same ordinance, you will own the tie of fellowship. It is a feeling which befits the occasion. Recognise your place in that community which is the body of Christ. This is an ordinance of joint privileges. 'The cup of blessing which we bless, is it not the communion [or joint participation] of the blood of Christ? The bread which we break, is it not the communion of the body of Christ? For we being many are one bread [or loaf] and one body; for we are all partakers of that one bread' (*1 Cor.* 10:16,17). The glow of mutual attachment should now be warm. 'Love as brethren;' (*1 Pet.* 3:8) and carry away this holy affection into your common life.

32. Cautions After Communion

After the first sacramental communion, the Apostles entered into temptation, fell asleep, and soon afterwards were guilty of greater sins. Let the young communicant be watchful against surprises. Even on the very day, the soul sometimes relaxes its vigour; as the bent bow flies back when unbound. Where the services are long, as is sometimes the case, there is a tendency to this result, from weariness of body and mind. Be exhorted to maintain seriousness and humility and quiet of soul, even though tears or rapture are denied you. What can more clearly indicate a shallow experience, if not a profane mind, than a speedy return to light reading, frivolous conversation, and worldly thoughts? Endeavour to preserve the sentiments which you have attained, and reflect upon the manner in which you have passed through this new and important scene of your life.

33. *Disappointed Hopes*

It is by no means unusual for persons to return from a first communion in deep distress. Instead of the peace and joy which they expected, they found only dullness, unbelief, and vexing thoughts. Or, at best, they received no addition of faith and emotion. In such cases, they are harassed with fears and even ready to abandon all hope. For the most part, these apprehensions are needless. The worst cases are those in whom there is no sense of dissatisfaction. The benefit of the communion is not always to be measured by its comforts. The graces of the Lord's Table are sovereign and manifold. They are not always productive of joy. There may be great advancement and true service of God, where there is no elation. The soul may be acceptable to Christ, where there are deep sorrows, or keen pangs of regret, or distressing self-condemnation. The ordinance has not been unfruitful, if it has left you low in the dust, convinced of your own remaining sin, helplessness, and need of Christ. But supposing that much was wrong in the frame of your spirit, what remains for you but to prostrate yourself anew at the feet of Jesus? Carefully review the nature of your preparation and mark its defects. Recall your mental acts during the sacrament; inquire what has been amiss; and resolve in God's strength to avoid these evils in time to come.

34. *Thankful Review*

Through the tender mercies of our God, there are many cases in which the young communicant retires from the Table of the Lord, strengthened and encouraged. The cardinal truth of Christianity has been set before his thoughts and becomes incorporated with his faith. He has seen Jesus (*John* 12:21). His views of the infinite freedom of salvation have been made more clear. The evidences of his acceptance with God have become brighter. He is more disposed than ever before, to yield himself as a sacrifice, soul, body and spirit, which is his reasonable service (*Rom.* 12:1). Where any part of this is true, you have new causes for gratitude. It is 'the Lord thy God which teacheth thee to profit' (*Isa*.48:17). Now is the time, to bless him for this grace, and to beg the continuance of it. Now is the time to set a watch against relapses, and to carry into effect the vows which you have made at the Lord's Table. In the future, you will look for the recurrence of this sacrament with a lively expectation, founded on experience.

35. *Going Down to the World*

The Lord's Supper has often been described as 'a mount of ordinances'. Such it often seems to the young communicant, who is disposed to say, with one of old, 'Master, it is good for us to be here' (*Mark* 9:5). But elevations like this are not for ever; and the descent from them is beset with temptation. It is a time of danger. Never will you need more circumspection. You are about to return to the very scenes of your former disobedience. How hard a task, to be a new character, amidst the old circumstances! Former allurements await you; former habits prepare their nets for you; former companions watch for your halting. The character of your whole future course depends very much upon the manner in which you sustain your new obligations. Cast yourself therefore, at the feet of infinite Wisdom and Grace, that you may be enabled to 'adorn the doctrine of God our Saviour in all things' (*Titus* 2:10).

36. Courage

'Be strong in the Lord, and in the power of his might' (*Eph.* 6.10). 'Quit yourselves like men!'(*1 Cor.* 16:13). Such injunctions are not obsolete. You are about to mingle with fellow-creatures, some of whom are at enmity with God. Reject with disdain the meanness of being ashamed of the faith. In every proper and humble way, let it be seen that you are a follower of Christ. Silence will sometimes be your duty; but 'be ready always to give an answer to every man that asketh you a reason of the hope that is in you, with meekness and fear?' (*1 Pet.* 3:15). Take care not to be talked out of your convictions; and arm yourselves with a constant faith in your ever-present Redeemer.

37. Interval Between Communions

There are some professing Christians who may be said to have only a sacramental piety. For a few days before and after the communion, they desist from gaieties, attend on devotions, and 'disfigure their faces' (*Matt.* 6:16). This done, they return with new zest to their covetousness or their pleasures. Do you need to be warned against this abuse? Perhaps not; and yet you may be in danger of a more refined hypocrisy. You may cease to be watchful and relax in faithfulness. Be it your solemn purpose to serve your Master both during the interval between communions as well as at the Lord's Table. So, when the approach of another communion is announced by the pastor, it will not be to you as it is to many, an unwelcome surprise.

38. Benefit of Frequent Communion

It is supposed, by many learned men, that the early Christians commemorated Christ's death at least every Lord's Day. In America there is a general disposition to celebrate this sacrament oftener than was customary with our forefathers. There are several classes of persons, to whom the Lord's Supper is peculiarly a source of strength and comfort. For example:
1. *Doubting Disciples*, who cannot have the free offer of grace and righteousness held out to them too often.

2. *Persons of Legal Views,* who are prone to dream of gaining merit. These mistakes are best corrected by going frequently to Gethsemane and Golgotha.

3. *Backsliders,* who are awakened by the call to self-examination, and melted when Jesus turns and looks upon them, as on Peter (*Luke 22:61*).

4. *Lonely Ones,* who need the cheering sense of fellowship, produced by this feast of brotherhood.

5. *Those in Trouble*, who ten thousand times have forgotten their earthly sorrows in the joys of Christ's presence.

6. *Such as are About to Die*, who need to prepare to pass over Jordan. The faith which the Communion demands is just the childlike trust which is suitable to the dying hour.

39. Subsequent Communions

A first communion is the most striking, but not always, perhaps not often, the most joyful or the most edifying. It is the privilege of true religion that its delights may go on increasing. Endeavour then to rise a step higher, on each successive occasion. Renew your self-examination and strive to gain clearer views of Christ.

40. Review of Numerous Sacraments

Should your life be spared so that you will have sat often at the Table of the Lord, there are some reflections which will be appropriate and useful. You will plainly have had great increase of light and privilege. Ask yourself then: 'How have I profited by these? What point have I reached in my spiritual pilgrimage? What evil habit have I broken? What besetting sin have I crucified? What holy principle has gained strength? What labours have I undertaken? What sacrifices have I made? How has my Christian progress agreed with what I hoped for? What special impulse have I derived from this last communion?'

41. Reasons Why Some Refrain from Partaking

There are instances of persons, long known as Christians, who allow the Lord's Supper to be celebrated without their participation. They give various reasons for this, three of which deserve to be considered as they are all too common..

1. 'I have failed to make preparation'.

If, with full knowledge of the coming ordinance, you have entirely neglected preparation of heart, you have sinned, and ought to repent. But this does not absolve you from your prior duty to Christ and his Church. In the brief period, therefore, which remains, cast yourself before God, and humbly go forward to his Table, relying on his forgiveness and aid. Let the same principle govern you, if, in travelling, you should find yourself unexpectedly present where the disciples of Christ are about to remember his death. Hezekiah's prayer is here applicable: 'The good Lord pardon every one that prepareth his heart to seek God, the Lord God of his fathers, though he be not cleansed according to the purification of the sanctuary' (*2 Chron.* 30:18–19).

2. 'I am not in charity with brethren'.

If you mean, that some person or persons may be expected to partake, between whom and yourself there is a feeling of malice – your duty is very plain because such a feeling is hateful to Christ. If you are the offended person, lose no time in pursuing the method enjoined by Christ (*Matt.* 18:15–20). If you are the offender, hasten to make confession and reparation. In either case, 'be reconciled to thy brother.' You commit a double sin by staying away from the Lord's Table on such a pretext. 'Therefore let us keep the feast, not with old leaven, neither with the leven of malice and wickedness, but with the unleavened bread of sincerity and truth' (*1 Cor.* 5:8).

3. 'I have lost my hope in Christ.'

Such language often proceeds from sincere believers, under the temporary hidings of God's face. But moods of feeling should not be made principles of action. Where a duty is definitely prescribed, we should not refuse to do it because of a great sense of unfitness, or we might as well abandon all the other means of grace. If therefore your declension has not reached the dreadful point, of your having renounced all profession of faith, it is clearly your duty to go to the Lord's Table. This temptation may be sent by Satan for the purpose of deterring you from this ordinance. This is a sacrament of which the very end is to exhibit Christ and so confirm faith. Come to it therefore, with new endeavours after repentance and with humble trust. If you find yourself impenitent, you have the highest motive to repent, but none to disobey your Lord. And while you will sin by partaking in unbelief, you will not escape sin by turning your back on the Lord's Table.

42. Seek the Sacramental Edification of Others

Selfishness insinuates itself into our best services. 'Look not every man on his own things, but every man also on the things of others' (*Phil.* 2:4). How rarely do we become concerned about the manner in which our friends and neighbours profit at the communion! Reformation on this point would tend to the revival of the churches. Seriously look around you, and consider who there are, properly within your reach, whom you may induce to employ those means which shall render this sacrament more edifying and more dear to them. By discreet counsels, by suitable books or tracts, and especially by the attraction of a holy spiritual example, you may be as an angel of mercy to some whom you love.

43. *Importance of Beginning Aright*

The importance of first steps, in any great undertaking, cannot be overrated. Although grace works some notable exceptions, it is generally true that men proceed as they have begun. This ought not to deter such as are conscious of past unfaithfulness from earnest repentance and reform, but it should afford you a powerful motive to begin aright. Beware of a low standard of religious character. Cherish a godly fear of taking your model from the majority of reputed Christians around you. The time at which you enter on your course is unfavourable in this respect, that there is, in the church, a prevalence of coldness, negligence, and conformity to the world. If you would reap the benefit of the labours of your calling, you will need to set a high standard, and to ask God's help, that you may make high attainments in grace the grand object of your life.

44. *The Post of A Young Christian*

Consider profoundly, I beseech you, your position, as one among the large number of young disciples. Older members of Christ's Church are every day leaving the field. Their places are to be taken by yourselves. The vast responsibilities, enterprises and toils of the coming day are to fall upon you. Others will soon look up to you, as you now look to your elders. The revolutions of time, though noiseless, are swift, and your working season is but a span. The Christianity of the next generation will take its degree and tone from the piety of those who are now girding on the armour. Therefore, whatever you regard as desirable to be attained hereafter, strive for now, with all the concentrated powers of your soul. Ask yourself, what measure of grace will fit you to be an example to others.

45. Blessedness of Youthful Profession

If indeed you have been effectually called, you have infinite cause of thanksgiving, that you have heard the voice of God in early life. It is an unspeakable blessing to be translated from darkness to light, at any age; but great and manifold are the advantages of having begun in spring. How striking are the words of Obadiah, 'I, thy servant, fear the Lord from my youth' (*1 Kings* 18:12). You have less to unlearn, than the aged, or even the mature. Your habits are less rigid. Your mind and heart are more susceptible of new impressions. If spared in life, you have a longer period of growth, and more time for bearing fruit. The embarrassments of the world have come upon you but partially. Your character is yet unformed and pliable.Let these be so many motives, to constrain you to arduous exertion to walk worthy of your vocation. And be assured, that if you look away from all misleading examples, even of seemingly good men, and fix our eye upon the life and teachings of the Lord Jesus, you will find your happiness increasing from hour to hour.

46. Principle of the Christian Walk

All your duties as a professing Christian may be arranged in three classes; those namely, which concern yourself, those which concern the Church, and those which concern the world at large. Of these, the first are the most important and indispensable and they are the source of all the rest. You are at present weak and inexperienced and your power to resist the evil influences of the world is as yet untested. Your spiritual enemies are numerous and mighty. Many have fallen in the very path on which you are now setting out. How great should be your concern to run the race that is set before you! To do this, you must possess an inward living principle, the author of which is the Holy Ghost. The all-important work therefore is within your own heart; the life of God in the soul. To this your first and constant attention must be directed – and you have already begun wrongly, if you put any thing external in the place of this.

47. Means of Self-Culture

Fellowship with God, who is the source of all strength, is kept up by the means of grace. These are channels of heaven's influence to the soul. Your proficiency will be in proportion to the faithful use of the exercises of private piety. Become cold and negligent in these and your uncertain progress can be easily predicted. You cannot live the life of God without communion with God in these acts. As faith is the spirit of other graces, so truth, which faith receives, must be constantly poured in to nourish the soul.

The depository of all saving truth is the Holy Scriptures. Go to this blessed volume daily, devoutly, and with delight. Be wary of every book which lessens your taste for the Bible. Begin from this hour to have a set time for the devotional reading of the Word, and another hour for the diligent study of its contents, in regular order. Write it upon your heart, as a sacred resolution, that all your life long you will maintain a loving familiarity with the oracles of God. And let your cry be, 'Open thou my eyes that I may behold wondrous things out of thy law!' (*Psa.* 119:18).

48. *Doctrinal Instruction*

Acquire early the habit of making yourself thoroughly familiar with all the truths of the Christian system, in their proper connection. Be not one of those who complain of doctrinal preaching and neglect doctrinal books. Sound doctrine is the food of faith. An experience without doctrine is like a house without walls, a body without bones, and a tree without root. So order your reading that it will never be long before you are studying some book on these subjects. Upon your accurate knowledge and hearty belief of evangelical doctrine will depend the solidity, symmetry, comfort, and fruitfulness of your Christian character.

49. Meditation

The duty of regular meditation is much neglected. Yet no one ever made high attainments in experience without it. This exercise is necessary to receive proper benefit from the Word. Seize opportune moments for serious, devout, continued thinking upon divine truth – such as the early morning, the twilight, the wakeful hours of night, and the Sabbath day. Pause now and ask yourself whether you have ever considered this as a duty, and whether you have ever practised it. Learn this art; sweeten your thoughts on retiring for the night with some good word of inspiration, and you will soon exclaim with gratitude, 'In the multitude of my thoughts within me, thy comforts delight my soul' (*Psa.* 94:19). The glorious person of the Lord Jesus should especially be the object of your fixed contemplation, after having sat at his table.

50. Prayer

Of all the means of grace, there is none which is more valuable than prayer, comprising the several parts of adoration, thanksgiving, confession, supplication, and intercession. Upon your knees and looking up into the compassionate face of your Heavenly Father, you are in that posture which above all others is most suited to the exercise of faith, hope, love, and every Christian grace. If you decline, the declension will commence just here. The maxim is true: 'Apostasy begins at the closet'. Let no slight reason satisfy you for having omitted your devotions just as you are not content with excuses for having omitted your necessary meals.

The evils to be avoided are forgetfulness, infrequency, irregularity, formality, wandering of mind, undue brevity, irreverence, coldness, and unbelief. Question yourself as to each of these points in particular. Beware of confining yourself to silent prayer, but in your regular devotions employ audible utterance because the voice has a great influence upon the feelings.

Have set times for prayer, at least every morning and evening; and, if possible, a set place for it. In accord with the admonition, 'Pray without ceasing' (*1 Thess.* 5:17), let your thoughts during the employments of the day often go up in ejaculatory prayer; which is so called because such aspirations are like arrows shot up towards heaven; and 'blessed is he that hath his quiver full of them'.

51. Daily Walk

'Seek first the kingdom of God and his righteousness' (*Matt.*6:33). In other words, make religion the leading and paramount concern of life. Is it so? 'Be thou in the fear of God, all the day long' (*Prov.* 23:17). To secure this, be sure to begin the day aright. Let your waking thoughts be heavenly and all the thinking of the day will be sweetened. Let your first employment be in devotion. Let your first reading be of God's holy Word compared with which the daily news and the interesting story are often seductive rivals. Recall your straying thoughts to God a thousand times a day during the paths of lawful duty. Take care to redeem time at night for self-examination and prayer. Thus you will learn to walk with God; and let me assure you that this lesson must be learnt in your early Christian life.

52. The Lord's Day

If your life is a busy one, you will find a sweet refreshment in the Sabbath. Except those hours which are bestowed on others, or on public worship, let it be your endeavour to spent the whole of the sacred time in acts of religious improvement. These may be sufficiently varied to prevent weariness or boredom but stories and diaries may absorb too many of these precious hours. You may measure your spirituality by the manner in which you habitually spend the Lord's Day. All eminent Christians have been remarkable for a conscientious use of this holy and blessed rest.

53. Outward Conduct

To lay down rules for external conduct would exceed our few pages. The divine rule is, 'As he which hath called you is holy, so be ye holy in all manner of conversation' (*1 Pet.* 1:15). Beginning with your nearest relations your obedience is to be shown in each of the widening circles of life. Above all, you should be the true Christian at home. Let it not be said of you that you manifest the least of the spirit of the Gospel to those who are nearest and dearest, such as parents, brothers, sisters, and companions. Pray that you may conduct the humblest part of daily business on Christian principles. 'Whatsoever therefore ye do in word or deed, do all in the name of the Lord Jesus, giving thanks to God and the Father, through him' (*Col.* 3:17).

54. The Family

The young communicant may also be the head of a family. Should this be your situation, you have a new circle of most tender and interesting duties. Souls, dearer to you than life, and dependants little less near, are looking up to you for Christian guidance and nurture. Your vows to God require that you should command your household, training them in the way of truth. You will not fail then to dedicate your beloved offspring to the Lord, from their very birth, and especially at their baptism. You will call your family together for the worship of God every morning and evening. It is painful to reflect, how many church members fail as to this plain and delightful duty. Surely they cannot have reflected on the inspired threatening: 'Pour out thy fury upon the heathen that know thee not, and upon the families that call not on thy name' (*Jer.* 10:25). Family religion which includes worship, instruction and government, is the necessary result of individual piety. If these are neglected, you cannot expect God's blessing.

55. Fashion and Amusement

The growing laxity of the age gives peculiar force to the exhortation, 'Be not conformed to this world' (*Rom.* 12:2). The rule of the majority is corrupt and dangerous; it is to do as others do. The consequence is mutual harm and perpetual declension in the Church. You will find professing Christians who, as they increase in wealth, constantly enlarge their liberty. It requires a keen eye to discriminate between their pleasures and purchases and those of the ungodly. Apply, if you can, the divine maxim, 'Love not the world, neither the things that are in the world; if any man love the world, the love of the Father is not in him' (*1 John* 2:15). The young communicant who is often asking how near he may go to the brink of sin and yet be safe, is near to his fall. Observe the families which have trod the path from ancient strictness to fashionable Christianity, and you will find their children one by one sliding away to looser forms of religion, if not to utter carelessness. The same principles apply to expenditure in dress, furniture, goods and luxurious living. 'Let your moderation be known unto all men' (*Phil.* 4:5).

56. Diligence

As a bondservant of the Lord Jesus Christ, yielded to him and no longer your own, you are zealously to do his work, every day of your life, and every hour of the day; 'not slothful in business, fervent in spirit, serving the Lord' (*Rom.* 12:11). It would be impossible to express too strongly the duty of living altogether for Christ. It is the entire business of life. There is no single lawful act, however menial or even despised, which may not be offered up to him. Thus, business and even labour become religious, and you spend every moment in the spirit of sacrifice. If you go down from the Lord's Table with this frame of mind, you are happy indeed.

57. Humility

The saying that nothing is more beautiful in a young Christian than humility is true. Pride was not made for man and it is especially hateful in one who has just come out of a state of condemnation. You may in some degree judge your spiritual condition by the low views which you entertain of yourself. It is a bad sign when a novice is puffed up, when he vaunts his own experience, thinks himself wiser than his elders, and is censorious towards brethren. 'Let each esteem others better than themselves' (*Phil.* 2:3). Lowliness of mind is at once an ornament and a protection; and hence the Apostle says, 'Be clothed with humility' (*1 Pet.* 5:5).

58. Duties to the Church

Besides those duties which, as has been said, primarily concern yourself, there are others which concern the Church of Christ and in the first instance that particular branch of it to which you have been united. In keeping with the explanation already given, you have not only made a profession of your individual faith but have joined a communion, in token of which you have partaken of the same loaf and the same cup. You are of this family. These are now your brethren and sisters in the Lord. No tie on earth is closer and your conduct should be such as to show that it is not a mere name. You henceforth owe them duties which are all fruits of holy love. For you are bound not only to Christ but to his people. Never cease to remember, that you are no longer your own, and that in some sort your individual interests are merged in those of the Christian body. You have entered on a walk which is not lonely, but social; therefore, 'Love the brotherhood' (*1 Pet.* 2:17).

59. Brotherly Love

While you have a sincere good will towards all the people of God, your more active affections must necessarily go forth to those who are next to you, those with whom you worship and join in sacramental communion; in other words, to your own church. These you are to 'love as brethren' (*1 Pet.*3:8). Is this the case in all our churches? Or is not the bond between member and member, no more in many cases, than that they sit in the same house and listen to the same preacher?

60. *Christian Acquaintance*

In order to practise this Christian fellowship and duty, what we greatly need is a more earnest attempt at mutual acquaintance. How can we help, or even love those whom we do not know? Yet how many who sit at the same sacramental table show elsewhere no sign of recognition? Plainly, the older members of a church should give the hand of invitation and welcome to the younger. The rich should abhor the thought of being ashamed of the poor. We may expect the curse of God upon our churches if this spirit prevails. And if advances are made, it must obviously be from the side of the more prosperous. Some of Christ's most favoured people, and some who might do you the most good, are among the poor of this world, who are 'rich in faith'. Study with diligence that passage of the Apostle James, in which he says, 'My brethren, have not the faith of our Lord Jesus Christ, the Lord of glory, with respect of persons' (*James* 2:1-9).

61. *Intimate Friends*

As Christianity does not forbid particular relationships, you will find great advantage in having a special circle of

Christian friends. Some or most of these will naturally be of your own age. But they should be selected upon a principle of mutual benefit. Absolute isolation is unfavourable to piety. Let the abundance of the heart sometimes flow forth to these persons, in discourse upon the great truths of the Gospel; and where circumstances favour it, join with them in acts of devotion. 'Iron sharpeneth iron; so a man sharpeneth the countenance of his friend' (*Prov.* 27:17).

62. Active Fellowship

The love of brethren is not an empty affection. It produces activity. If the spirit of Christ dwells in you, it will be your delight to help and relieve afflicted brethren. You will early begin to seek out sufferers, and will find your way to the doors of the poor, the diseased, the widow, and the orphan. Above all, you will watch for occasions for conveying some spiritual encouragement or comfort to those who need it.

63. Aid to the Gospel

One of the most obvious duties which you owe to the Church is the support by all means within your reach of a gospel worship and ministry . If all the members of a communion are true of heart in regard to this point, the work will probably go forward successfully, however small the number. By enrolling yourself in the member-ship, you have pledged yourself to take your share of the burdens. More may be justly expected of you than of the world. The support of the pastor, especially if the flock is small, should weigh on your heart. And every undertak-ing for building up the spiritual house, should have your help and your prayers. Enter the ranks with the resolution to be a working member.

64. *Attendance on Worship*

Set it before you, as a duty for life, to give regularly and fitting attendance on the worship of the sanctuary, every Lord's Day. Let not your place be vacant. Consider punctuality in attendance as one of your duties to Christ. It is not superfluous to say, let your demeanour be rever-ent. Be not one of those young communicants – such alas! there are - who, instead of a holy silence, spend the moments before the actual commencement of the service in conversation. Even though the words were of spiritual things, this is not the place or occasion for them. What preparation is so seemly as the solemn stillness and hushed expectation of a whole assembly! It must be lamentable that this is wanting in some of our churches. Aid your pastor by kind words and by prayer, rather than by flattery, or by attempts to disparage others in his behalf. The best friends of a pastor are not those who visit him with adulation and fondly suppose that the precious gospel can do them good from no lips but his. Therefore be not unwilling sometimes to see another in his place. Consent that the gifts which are constantly yours should now and then be enjoyed by others. Do not pay him the doubtful compliment of choosing the occasion of his absence to leave your own church. Hearken to the lessons which he teaches, and do your part to carry out in practice all his scriptural plans. Cultivate his acquaintance, and while you hold his time to be precious, do not doubt his willingness at all seasons to converse with you on the concerns of the soul. In the worship of God's house, remember that you are more than a listener or a witness. Bear your part, mentally in prayer, and vocally in praise.

65. *Weekly Meetings*

In fully organised congregations, there is usually a religious service during the week. The preparation for this costs your pastor a certain amount of care and labour. Let not this be despised. No aid, which can be universally rendered, is more cheering to his heart than constant attendance at this meeting. However it may be neglected and undervalued by the majority of people, establish it as a rule that you will hold up his hands by your presence. You will there be sure to meet the more spiritual members of the church; you will extend the limits of Christian acquaintance, and will receive knowledge and edification. It is hardly needful to add, that every conscientious church member will so order the arrangements of his family, his visits, and his social recreations, as not to conflict with the regular meetings of the church. The remarks just made are applicable, with slight qualification, to the weekly prayer meeting.

66. *Love of Souls*

The whole appearance of things would be altered in the Church if each of its members could be possessed with a sense of his obligation to make individual efforts for the conversion of souls. This is often left to ministers and church officers. Yet every man has some circle of influence, and some laymen have been instruments in bringing hundreds to the knowledge of the truth. 'Brethren, if any of you do err from the truth, and one convert him; let him know, that he which converteth the sinner from the error of his way shall save a soul from death, and shall hide a multitude of sins' (*James* 5:20).

67. *Sunday Schools*

Sunday schools have at least doubled the working power of every church in which they are well established. The energetic members of any Christian society are commonly Sunday school teachers, or have been such. Employment in this work is usually the first labour which a young disciple ventures to undertake. The whole business of the Sunday school tends to promote the spirit of benevolence and the habit of beneficence. Every order of talent may here find a place.

68. Charities

Every congregation has within itself certain associations for benevolent purposes and these are sometimes composed of Christian women. But the number of truly active members is commonly very small. Various reasons, often unworthy and frivolous, if not connected with the 'pride of life', keep many who might render effective aid from uniting in these labours of love. The object may be the contribution of means for charity, or the making of garments for the suffering, or the neglected work of visiting the sick or poor, the 'fatherless and widows in their affliction' (*James* 1:27). Whatever be the end sought, let no proud reserve or carping objection keep you from having a share in it. You cannot begin too soon to exercise yourself in actual and personal well-doing which is much more rare than the giving of alms through others.

69. Edification of Brethren

Feeling yourself in fellowship with the body of believers, you will naturally own your obligation to do all that in you lies to promote the holiness of every other Christian. To indicate methods for this would be to write a volume. The great point is, to have the desire and intention to do so. Is this the tendency of your mind, and does it show itself in your daily prayers and endeavours?

70. Scandals

'It is impossible but that offences will come, but woe unto him through whom they come' (*Luke* 17:1). For an offence, scandal or stumblingblock, to have taken place in the scriptural sense, some degree of public knowledge of it is essential. But it is also true that a large measure of guilt belongs to him who extends that circle by talking about the sins of brethren. Almost every church has some mischievous tongue of this sort. Profound silence would often prevent the spread of dishonourable reports. The rule is as old as Moses: 'Thou shalt not go up and down as a talebearer among thy people' (*Lev.* 19:16). Abhor the slightest approach to this hateful practice. Be tender of the reputation of a brother, and where you can not deny an evil report, at least show how truly you dislike it. 'The north wind driveth away rain: so doth an angry countenance a backbiting tongue' (*Prov.* 25:23).

71. Peace Making

To promote harmony and love in the church is a Christlike employment. Differences continually arise among brethren and they are abominable in the sight of God. Not only should you avoid them yourself but you should spare no pains to prevent and heal them in others. There is scarcely a feud or a coldness which might not be removed in its commencement. But the trickling rill soon swells to a torrent. 'The beginning of strife is as when one letteth out water' (*Prov.* 17:14). Timely intervention between the contending parties, with honest and affectionate entreaty, will in most cases be successful. 'Blessed are the peacemakers, for they shall be called the children of God' (*Matt.* 5:9).

72. *Reproof*

The church-covenant implies not only mutual love but mutual watchfulness. How much better is it to tell a brother's fault to himself than to tell it to others? Sin in our brethren should give us great pain and we should use unceasing efforts to correct it. But no duty requires more circumspection and heavenly wisdom. Conducted aright, charitable reproof seldom fails sooner or later to be useful. 'He that rebuketh a man afterwards shall find more favour than he that flattereth with the tongue' (*Prov.* 28:23). Indifference to the spiritual progress of our companions is a sin which is forbidden by the spirit of that Levitical law, 'Thou shalt not hate thy brother in thine heart; thou shalt in any wise rebuke thy neighbour, and not suffer sin upon him' (*Lev.* 19:17). It is the opposite of holy love.

73. *Duties to the World*

Only Christianity teaches the true brotherhood of mankind. 'Thou shalt love thy neighbour as thyself', is the second table of the Law. And if you ask, who is my neighbour? the reply of our Lord in a beautiful parable is, that your neighbour is he whom Providence throws within the reach of your help. Henceforth it should be your purpose to do all that is within your power for the temporal and spiritual good of all your fellow men.

74. *Modesty in Labours*

How hard it is to strike the happy medium between selfish inaction and over-busy zeal! 'Wisdom is profitable to direct' (*Eccl.* 10:10). Forwardness, and officious bustle are especially displeasing in a young Christian. You will be most likely to pursue the right path, if your daily efforts to do good are tempered with humility. When you are in doubt as to ways of being useful, you should add to your prayers a resort to the counsel of aged and experienced advisers.

75. *Seeking Opportunities*

Where there is a will, there will be a way. Earnest desire to do good will certainly suggest methods. Some have a peculiar faculty for devising happy schemes, which may afterwards be practised by themselves or others. It is well for the mind to be teeming with plans of usefulness. He is but a slothful servant, who always lies still till the summons of some urgent duty is brought to his door. Accustom yourself to go out in search of occasions for honouring Christ in the person of his suffering people.

'To do good and to communicate, forget not, for with such sacrifices God is well pleased' (*Heb.* 13:16). Place often before your mind, the tribunal of the Last Day, and shudder lest the Son of Man should say to you, 'Inasmuch as ye did it not to the least of these, ye did it not to me' (*Matt.* 25:45).

76. *The Spread of the Word*

Happy would it be, if every member of every communion should, from the first, feel himself charged with a part of the great duty of extending the means of salvation in all the region around him by the founding or sustaining of new churches. Your eye should be kept on this. You my render help by counsels and plans, by contribution, and, in some circumstances, by personally casting in your lot with struggling brethren. Large churches should aid those which are small. Some congregations are far too large. Timely additions from these to small undertakings may be as life from the dead. Think seriously on the delightful retrospect of a church established by yourselves and others, having thrown your services into the work at the critical moment.

77. *Liberality*

Hold yourself ready to contribute to every good enterprise, according to your ability. However small your gift may be, remember the widow's two mites, and that 'it is accepted according to that a man hath and not according to that he hath not' (*2 Cor.* 8:12). Give alms of such things as you have, and you will find your means increase. For 'God is able to make all grace abound towards you; that ye always having all sufficiency in all things may abound to every good work' (*2 Cor.* 9:8).

78. *Systematic Giving*

The poor give more in proportion than the rich. As men grow in wealth few of them keep up the rate of their contribution to the Lord's treasury; whereas they ought to increase it. This evil will be avoided, if you adopt the rule of setting aside a stated portion of your income. Such was the method recommended in a certain case by the apostle Paul: 'Upon the first day of the week let every one of you lay by him in store, as God hath prospered him, that there be no gatherings when I come' (*1 Cor.* 16:2).

79. *Personal Giving*

All men find it easier to give money than to give their actual services. Yet these are the most important and the most delightful acts of mercy. Begin at once to seek out cases of suffering. The most deserving are those which will never come to you. Accustom yourself to minister to the poor who are sick. Shrink not from any self-denial involved in interesting other benevolent persons in objects of charity. But by no means forego the sacred and self-rewarding duty of going yourself to the house of need or of mourning. 'Pure religion [the word means *religious service*] and undefiled before God and the Father is this, to visit the fatherless and widows in their affliction, and to keep himself unspotted from the world' (*James* 1:27).

80. *Conclusion*

If the world is to be converted, and the Church made glorious, within any short period, there must be a great regard for piety in those who are now young Christians. Much depends on having a high standard of personal holiness. Be persuaded that there are heights of grace, attainable even on earth, which have not been reached by you, or by the majority of believers. Direct your prayers and efforts to the acquisition of every Christian virtue, agreeably to the admonition of Paul: 'Finally, brethren, whatsoever things are true, whatsoever things are honest, whatsoever things are just, whatsoever things are pure, whatsoever things are lovely, whatsoever things are of good report; if there be any virtue, and if there be any praise, think on these things' (*Phil.* 4:8).

'O Jesus, my Saviour! thy blessed humanity, impress it on my heart! Make me most sensible of thy infinite dignity, and of my own vileness, that I may hate myself as a thing of nought, and be willing to be despised and trodden upon by all as the vilest mire of the streets; that I may still retain these words, – I AM NOTHING, I CAN DO NOTHING, AND I DESIRE NOTHING BUT ONE' (*Archbishop Leighton*).